Leave The Dreaming To The Flowers

Tiffiny Rose Allen

Leave The Dreaming To The Flowers

Copyright © 2022 Tiffiny Rose Allen

All rights reserved. This book or any portion thereof may not be reproduced or used in any manner whatsoever without the express written permission of the author except for the use of brief quotations in a book review.

Printed in the United States of America

First printing, 2017

ISBN-13:
9798846147423

For the ones who continue, in spite of it all.

"It takes a great deal of courage to see the world in all its tainted glory, and still to love it."
~Oscar Wilde

INTRODUCTION

Five years sure does fly by fast, doesn't it? I remember when I first closed my notebook, the final page ink filled, the magenta faux leather encasing several years' worth of pages. I told myself that I was going to take the leap and put my first "real" book together. I never thought five years later I would have several more collections out, and that I would be where I am now. I guess a lot of people could say that about a lot of different things, and I guess I consider myself lucky for being able to say them. Writing has truly been my safe haven and my peace of mind. No matter what I am going through in life, being able to pick up a pen or type in my notes app has allowed me to process whatever is happening or even not happening.

I like to think our unique creative processes choose us when we need them most, whether that is to guide us to something bigger or simply be a way to process and cope with the challenges and beautiful tangents of life. This book, and all of the other books that I have written, are my views of the world.

These poems are my perspective on womanhood, on the beginnings of my spiritual journey, on how things are around me, and no matter what those things might be, I have been determined to make them into something beautiful.

I will always be thankful for the words that I have been fortunate enough to share with you all, and I am beyond grateful for anyone and everyone who has chosen to read them. I have always told myself that if my words reach just one person who resonates with them and maybe gains some hope from them, then my job is considered finished.

To be quite honest, I write rather selfishly. I like seeing my work on a bookshelf, whole and complete. Something that I have realized though, is that just because a book is bound and placed neatly on a shelf, does not mean that it is finished and complete.

I have decided to revisit this work, not just because it is turning five years old this August of 2022, but because I feel both like I was an entirely different person when I wrote it, and also because I somehow feel exactly the same too.

I use a lot of flower imagery in my work and its representation. It wasn't really a deliberate thing that I had intended, it just kind of came to me and I ran with it. Flowers have always shown me that beauty can be found absolutely anywhere, in the most unlikely and random places. They can bloom and sprout between cement or be tenderly cared for in gardens, they are able to withstand the rain and wind. Flowers are gorgeously delicate yet they persevere. People can stomp on them and trample them, gift them in bouquets for salutations and love offerings. No matter what they go through, they remain beautiful throughout it all. Flowers always come forward in one way or another, holding our dreams and our desires for us.

Through the years, the world has remained both unpleasant and kind somehow, we all have found things to inspire us and not inspire us, we have all learned and done the best that we could do, and in so many ways, and at the end of it all, we continue.

I hope this edition and reworking of my first poetry collection is something that you can enjoy on a nice day outside, maybe sitting under a tree, next to some water, and I hope somewhere close by you can see some wildflowers blooming, letting you know that you are right where you need to be. These poems are shared for the sole intent of letting you know that you are not alone in anything.

Signed,
Tiffiny Rose Allen
(Your friend)

Part I

~Author's Note~
This section depicts poems about mundane reality, emotions that we feel as days go on, strong and simple, fierce and gentle. The many complexities tied into everything and nothing.

Containing

People At The Store **1**

Society's Dictionary **4**

Simple Things **6**

Pondering **9**

Now **11**

Wilted Flowers **14**

We Will **16**

Hope Remains **18**

Maybe **20**

Precious **21**

Melody **22**

I Will Never Let You Go **24**

Body And Soul **27**

Let Be **30**

So Many Questions Part I **32**

So Many Questions Part II **33**

So Many Questions Part III **35**

Lies Of Truth **37**

Two Words **38**

Depression **41**

Getting Through The Maze **43**

~

Should we go back to the beginning and
restart?
I gazed and I saw flower petals resting near the moon.

~

People At The Store

There are three distinct types of people who stand in line at the grocery store.

The first,

went in to buy a full shopping basket of food

around ten or eleven in the morning

and were able to check out all in due time

and be on their merry way

to carry on with their day.

The second,

didn't get a chance to go shopping

until later in the day, so they are bound to rush around and

when they finally get to the checkout

Leave The Dreaming To The Flowers - Tiffiny Rose Allen

they end up using three different credit cards

because their bills came out of their accounts that day

so, they take about an hour to finish their purchase.

Then

there's the third.

They're the ones who needed to get two things

and the only checkout line that happens to be open

is the one with the Second.

So, they wait a grand amount of time

for the Second shopper to check out

standing impatiently

knowing their time is being wasted away.

Everyone rushing in and rushing out

in a frenzy, got to hurry.

No one is inadequate, and no one is wrong,

Leave The Dreaming To The Flowers - Tiffiny Rose Allen

their experiences just merely causing reflections.

One, two, and three—

different time zones

and different dimensions

numbers of life stirring rapidly

all in a random conjunction—

Walking past each other's salvation and betrayal

as carts roll along imitation marble.

Getting food to last the day

'cause let's face it

none of those potato chips are going to make it to tomorrow.

Society's Dictionary

I thought I knew the difference between right and wrong, but I couldn't hear the instructor speaking to me.

I know the capital of Alaska, but I don't know where my name went.

I know the difference between a parrot and a parrotlet, but I don't know where my name went.

Is karma going to come for me tonight?

Is it going to recount every wrong turn and scratch and put them in a bag marked with a bright yellow pen?

I can remember the capital of Alaska but I can't remember my own name.

Juneau, Alaska, right?

I haven't even been to Alaska yet.

What am I looking for?

I know what my name is—

I just don't have a meaning for it.

What is this name's place?

What is it for?

I'm searching for the meaning

I wonder if it's gone or if it is just hiding.

All the distinct species of parrots, they all have their own names,

parrotlets are smaller, but they're all more vibrant in their color.

Maybe definitions left today,

went to lunch or took a vacation

because I can't find myself in the dictionary—

You know the one, the one that tells us what we're supposed to be doing and how we're supposed to be okay with it.

Simple Things

The simple things, why do they happen?

You cry

you get a napkin

you laugh

you get a smile.

You hurt

you get punished

you help

you get rewarded.

Sometimes no one notices

sometimes they just turn their head.

Sometimes you get a caring friend

other times you get a selfish fool.

The simple things,

why do they happen?

Ask

you get an answer,

aim

you get to fire.

Try to speak

you get hushed,

try to smile,

you get frowns.

Are things simple?

Don't they happen?

You don't always notice

you don't always care,

you can't always receive.

Is it worth the argument?

Is fighting over something silly

worth the words?

Is crying over something loved

not worth the tears?

If you care hard enough to realize,

then why do you wait to take your right action?

Why do I write if words are left unread?

The simple things

they happen, they have a purpose,

they matter.

Pondering

What is this poetry that fills me?

What causes me to write these words?

To think these thoughts

and to live this life?

What is the foundation what is the core?

So many questions and I'll keep asking more.

I wonder what caused me to choose that book

why I took a liking to that show,

why those paintings make me feel emotional.

Maybe I am not the one who chose those things

maybe they chose me

but why would they want to choose me?

Why would the universe choose to place this soul

in the path of all that lives?

Is it selfish of me to ask?

All things might not have an answer,

But I think there is still relevance in asking the question.

Now

You're still here

I'm still here

what we waited for has not yet come.

Could we wait longer,

perhaps just a little longer?

You've always looked

but you never tried

was it vague

was it wrong?

Did I have it unsung?

Whispering shores and hidden runes

nobody cares about today

they only shout 'Tomorrow! We'll do it all tomorrow!'

What about now?

Don't people care about now?

Now's the time to see the sunrise

now's the time to smile

now's the time to sing what's been unsung

do what's been undone.

Live your ways free

live your ways now

for now is all we have.

always expecting things

always wanting things

never loving what we have now.

There are so many things to do now.

take a rest if you need to, then let's get started.

Wilted Flowers

The sun shone so brightly

it blinded the eyes,

the flowers wilted by its shine.

Nevertheless, the clouds came and tamed the sun

pouring down the rain

making the flowers tall again

the people able to see, not blinded

their eyes could see the rain, now.

Then the rain stopped

and the moon came out

making the night so calm,

causing the flowers to sleep.

If a flower can sleep,

we can find our tired eyes and lay our heads

upon a pillow.

If a flower can regain its strength, so can we.

If flowers can wilt and feel so sad to the touch,

we can pick them up and plant them

somewhere safe,

for we have wilted once.

We Will

My laughter has faded

my smile is gone.

Your hope still stands

my hope still stands

our hope still stands

We will not ease their demands

we will not cease and let be

we will have victory,

we shall conquer,

not be hushed

but be free

from all that is against you and me.

We will laugh again, friend

won't we?

Hope Remains

You mistook my ways of good

for ways of bad

You believe that I stood

on only things that we once had.

You've no idea how much it pains me

to know you think such things.

I have tried to step pass,

all the things that no longer last,

but only haunt me on some days now.

I want to escape, be free

to breathe air without worrying about it

to live life without sorrows and fears,

to find my safety

so that I know I'll be far from snares,

and be only with those who care.

The day will come

my friend, my fate

when I will be far from my injured slate.

Maybe

If life were what it should be

then what would humanity come to?

Would we still climb mountains

and tell our precious tales,

or would we be forgotten,

and our lives nothing but soundless wails?

~

Pray tell dear, what is it that life "should" be then?

Is it merely our projection of perfection?

Precious

A new age, a new place

trying to hide from the stage,

my heart seems to race.

Home may be far

I look upon a star

but I know I'll come this way again.

I know I'll be home again.

And my troubles will lessen

my smiles will multiply

I'll find joy in simple things

be farther from one that stings

make each day a precious one

and never sit too long in the sun.

Melody

Thoughts of being irrelevant have entered my mind again.

It is almost like a cycle,

it comes and it goes

it brings me down and then dissipates.

When I start to feel good again, doubt sets in,

Why is my mind like this?

The changing of the stars, the constellations

Mercury in its retrograde,

playing with my thoughts.

'Tis a strange melody

that gets played again and again.

Listen to one song too often,

Filed down fingernails play a note

soft touch on piano keys

don't forget to keep up with the melody.

Steadfast horizon,

don't give in to doubt

fight the current and forget the chaos of the water.

Life will drag you from shore to shore,

but it is up to us to decide if it matters.

Let life take you where it will go,

'cause something good could be waiting.

I Will Never Let You Go

I've been scared a couple of times

Big and trivial things have frightened me,

but how am I to calm myself

when there's so little I can trust?

Please don't betray me

there's so much I want you to see.

How am I going to tell

what is real and what is not

if everything I love gets full of hate?

How am I going to move on?

How am I going to lift my feet?

If the ground is too overwhelmed

how will I learn to run?

Briars and thorns enwrap me

oh, what am I going to do

when I'm still not sure if I can trust you?

Please

don't betray me.

Fights and misunderstandings

they change our views of things,

though shit may rise

and you'll despise

I will never let you go.

Even if our dreams fail

and the skies above us rain down hail

And even if the others don't learn to love

If all their lives they scream and yell

I won't ever let you go.

I will hold you until we rise, together.

No matter what may lay ahead

I will never let you go.

Body And Soul

A flaw can be something great

it can bleed

it can interrogate.

It can consume your every pore

make you cry and demand something more.

A flaw can make you hate yourself

you'll wish for photoshop to erase your scars

you'll look at plastic people and want to live a plastic life

cause even though your skin is impure

you realize that your soul has been tapped by the unholy.

Your plasticized affair is to be taken up with God

you don't want your life to be more odd.

These marks on my skin have been with me for years

Leave The Dreaming To The Flowers - Tiffiny Rose Allen

When my body was fifteen

I was nervous in my head

thinking my iniquity was so great that it had burst through my skin.

The marks that hug my face

have been my childhood friends

one was from the table

one was from the desk.

My running and climbing have become my facial crest.

My stomach is not flat

I felt like I could not wear anything daring

Without looks at a pudgy belly and marks on thighs.

The lines that protrude become a web of mistakes that I can't undo.

Mind was racing with paranoia

so many that vanquish my trust

Seems like all they want to do is control you

it feels like my heart's going to bust.

Made me feel like a coward

I'll curl up in a ball and devour myself.

I am told that I am beautiful

I know I need to love myself completely.

Our lives are too ruled to be wasting our time

if you find yourself beautiful

then don't let anyone criticize the love you have,

for you.

Remember beauty is not body

beauty is your soul.

Strength is not how heavy you can lift

it's when you find your bravery.

Let Be

The day was full of grace

was full of laughter in this place.

Quite pleasant as the sun shines high

clouds of joy up in the sky

who knows how tomorrow will be

perhaps it is a catastrophe

A lump, a log, an epiphany,

whatever it will be

we will face it strongly

we will be ready, no matter how long.

A star

a moon

a blazing light

we will fret no more about the day tonight

because tomorrow will come

when you open your eyes.

So Many Questions

Part I

Hey there, you

What are you doing there, alone?

Why hasn't someone

come along and swept you away?

What are your secrets?

Your dreams and receipts?

Why is that internal monologue

so low and so loud?

Could she be a part of your thoughts?

Questions, I know, so many questions

but

could she be,

a part of your thoughts?

So Many Questions

Part II

You held her hand

in your mind,

and she held yours too.

Hype up the vows

make a certain promise

you didn't follow through.

Didn't matter to the girl

She loved you anyway.

No gift or word could compare

If she knew she was loved.

All would be well

If she knew she was loved.

To show affection everyday

to someone you care for

can be hard

even if some people voice it's not.

Anything worth having

is going to be filled with difficult tasks

a kiss on the cheek has a thousand words.

She can't put her arms around you

she's too far away

she lets you know she's there to hear your thoughts

but you're turning them all to the back

turning them away to the depths of your mind.

So Many Questions

Part III

She dives into her poetry,

he dives into his cars,

she writes out her thoughts, fears, faiths.

He works out the rusted screws,

and cleans up the dents and scratches,

with precision and great care.

No words spoken,

only written and thought upon.

She doesn't like feeling like a piece of caution tape.

He doesn't know how to comfort her

if she does not use her words.

That is all they have right now.

Words and words and words and words.

Leave The Dreaming To The Flowers - Tiffiny Rose Allen

Open a wound and see a reaction,

is it one of love,

or is it one of nonchalance?

Once wounds get opened,

they do not easily get closed

and in opening such things

views can be forever altered.

Hate to rehash the past,

but you can't keep it locked up forever.

And you didn't,

it's out.

Lies Of Truth

To turn to something false

something that will never live,

fills our hearts with joy

until we realize what we've done.

Why does fiction rule our life?

Why do lies want to become the truth?

Well, to put it simply

we tell our truths

through the lies that we write,

the lies that we read

the lies that we wish

the lies we hold our hope to,

cling to, and suffer with.

Leave The Dreaming To The Flowers ~ Tiffany Rose Allen

Two Words

Damp hair

Good song

Don't share

Too long.

April's veins

May's blood

Paper planes

A rosebud.

Smile consumed

Day's gone

Flower's bloom

Soul pawn.

Maybe later,

Just today

Money saver

The prepay.

Checkered flannel

Don't hype

Awkward panel

A mistype.

Better yet

Live away

Don't let

Sorrow stay.

Missed message

Downward eyes

New passage

Small lies.

Sweet silhouette

How fair.

Slight reject

So unaware.

It's cool.

Depression

They said it was fine and dandy,

but it's not fine and dandy.

I sit here feeling like a piece of candy,

while everyone is crying

and inside I feel like dying,

because I'm not so sweet

I don't know how to make ends meet,

I don't know how to comfort or even to begin,

I feel like I'm tumbling in my sin.

Identities are cracking,

and

they sit around and make me feel like I'm laughing

because I don't have the right words to comfort.

I don't have the right words to go along with your thoughts today.

My centimeter of thoughts waver,

I am not a lifesaver.

All I can do is sit and look like candy,

while you tell me that everything is fine and dandy.

Getting Through The Maze

                            Stars shoot over the dark turned sky

                        and down below some children cry.

Where do we begin in this maze?

It is here where everyone stays.

                        Not all are strong, not all are weak

                          most are silent, most don't speak.

Waiting here is where we stand

across the bridges,

across the land.

                Try to purge all sin and hate

         try to focus on getting a clean slate.

                        No one listens, no one knows

              of all the dangers and all the crows.

They will run and they will cry

but we will stand here until we say goodbye.

                                        Shooting stars, up in space

                                                all entwined

                                        fit together like lace.

                We will stand here, yes right here

          and none of us will shed a tear.

No this isn't war, yet it is a fight

Stubborn 'til we see the light.

                              When the sun shines down,

                                    we will never frown

                                        we will explain

                            all the joys and all the pain.

'Tis here we stand

looking down at the sand.

No, it's not perfect,

not one bit

but this is where we'll claim our home.

This imperfect peace is where we'll sit.

Leave The Dreaming To The Flowers - Tiffiny Rose Allen

Part II

~Author's Note~

The poems in this section center around friendship, a little more closely on the ending of friendships and the many emotions that come with it. Friends and loved ones can be the greatest joys in our lives, and sometimes, circumstances lead to friendships ending or being put on the sidelines. This isn't necessarily anyone's fault, but we often can't help how we feel when these things happen, and it is always better to feel through it and process it all, then to simply ignore it and pretend that the ache is not there.

Leave The Dreaming To The Flowers - Tiffiny Rose Allen

Containing

Weathered Time **50**

And, Scene **52**

A Best Friend **54**

Bittersweet Letter **57**

Flood **60**

I.Miss.I.Love.I.Miss.You **62**

I Hate It When… **65**

Try **68**

The Progression Of Friendship **69**

Flaws **75**

White Clouds **76**

Time **78**

Here **80**

Earth Remains **82**

A Storm **84**

Letting Go And Walking Forward **86**

~

It feels like the words I wrote in the past just come back to haunt me.

I've taken this lesson again and again.

This time I'm numb to it. Maybe this time I've learned.

Maybe this time they will not come back again, they will only serve as reminders for all I've grown through.

~

Weathered Time

Friendship was held before you rang the bell,

then the sound

pulled through the air

suddenly

time disappeared between us two

and I moved on and walked away

trying to avert my eyes.

I looked back a time or so

but I did not pursue

because in my mind

I knew.

You were a force not to be walked with again.

You were my friend,

Leave The Dreaming To The Flowers - Tiffiny Rose Allen

You were,

yet now you are

no longer.

And, Scene

Flecks of gold fall from my eyes

                                      it's so scary with all these lights.

Times of comfort

                                        times of pain

we keep on

                                      traveling this lane.

                        I can't express the ways of my heart

                                  I look clean

                                  I look the part

on a stage now

                                      time to play

every reason on Earth to delay

yet still we carry on

                                      still, we carry on

                seems that's the only way

                come at me what may

I won't stay bound by

 worded chains

or slandering persona.

                I'll find a way to stop the stage.

A Best Friend

You are a ray of delight

you make all drunken days sober.

When my world begins to crumble

there you are

helping me put the falling structures back up.

Not the structure of solitude,

not of sadness or sin.

The structure of freedom

that let's no evil one in.

You put my mind at ease

my silent torments are pushed into the shadows.

You are a stress reliever

a painkiller

you are one of those good drugs,

And when those are all run out

I'll still have you.

You'll become the sun

you'll shine on the moon

and the moon will be amongst the stars.

Stars so bright,

they'll cover our scars.

I'll be there for you,

no matter, no care.

Like water, like hail

I'll come crashing in

wave after wave

until you are whole again.

We'll be by each other's sides

No matter how far apart we'll be.

Oceans, mountains, volcanoes, screw that.

A best friend cannot be stopped by the earth.

You,

are my best friend.

Let's go and defy it all

and be invincible to the world.

Bittersweet Letter

I remember when you sent me letters

and I so impatiently waited

so excited for one to arrive.

We would talk on and on

barely have time to breathe.

Then gradually,

the words began to wither

shortening until there were no more.

Our breaths became steadier,

I sent the last letter over a month ago

and now it's your turn to reply.

I wonder if I began to bore you

If my life just became irrelevant to you.

You haven't grown old to me

Leave The Dreaming To The Flowers - Tiffiny Rose Allen

I still wait for your letter

only more patiently.

I still wait for that sound on my phone

hoping that the next message will be from you.

So much, I do.

If we are not to reunite

I shan't forget our light.

We were so, so bright

we walked on the stars

and we traveled to Mars

we teleported tacos too.

You were, and I hope possibly

That you still will be

my precious friend whom I love, dearly.

Walk out of the dark

and take my hand

"Are you back?" I will think

and the look in your eye

will tell me so.

Flood

I thought I was okay

but it turns out I'm not.

Yet again I face this maze alone.

My sidekick has left again

here I stand, alone

all my problems

all my complaints

face me in a flood.

I don't know how to swim

yet I don't want to drown.

Must keep on kicking my legs

keep my head above the waters

I mustn't let this liquid consume me,

for if it does prevail

I will have no chance

at breathing air, again.

I.Miss.I.Love.I.Miss.You.

If I tell you that I miss you

that won't cut you to your core.

If I tell you that I love you

an overused phrase that you'll ignore.

I tried my best to hold your hand

I thought I was hanging on

yet when I looked 'twas only the glove from your hand

an empty shell towards the dawn.

For whatever it is worth

when I speak those phrases two

a shout to the whole earth

I do, I really do

undeniably, miss you.

We were more than just good friends

our conversations dove too deep

talk on until the day ends

it was so hard for us to sleep.

Constant compliments

maybe they wore thin

our letters soaked in pain and candy

we spoke so loud but

on the floor, you hear a pin.

To others, I seem fine and dandy

but you knew my true soul.

I'll never forget the times

when you knew me honest and whole

broken but still whole.

You showed me your true self

so I thought anyway,

now I can't reach the top shelf

farther you sailed, away.

It's been nearly a year,

well just quite,

since I first opened up to you

and I say with all my might

I say it again, again.

I

miss

I

love

I

miss

you.

and I forgive you

for fading away from me.

I Hate It When...

I hate it when people change their minds

when people distract you with methods of all kinds

when people decide to leave you

for no reason at all

when people cause you to fall.

When people lie to your face

when people think it is okay to replace

when they use acts of violence and start a war

when they ignore the hungry and the poor

when they stop admiring the flowers

I hate it when people are too scared to be themselves

and don't reveal their own powers.

I hate when people tell you

that they dearly, dearly love you

Leave The Dreaming To The Flowers - Tiffiny Rose Allen

then show you their affection

by staring you down like an investigation.

I hate when people say

That you never ever talk

That you act like nothing happened

And just continue to walk.

I hate when you want to speak, try to speak

say something and they throw your words to dirt.

Look at this torn shirt

look at this tear-stained massacre that's been

sewn too many times

never fully healing.

I hate when the one thing you want to say is thrown away.

"It's safer when I shut my mouth." I say.

"It's safer when I talk too much." I say.

It's better when I don't deal with this mutiny with you.

I can't deal with it with you.

I hate when they judge every act that you do

like you're on a stage, all eyes on you.

I hate it, a lot.

More than not

who I'm around determines my mood

Kind. Malign. Rude.

Just let things go as they go

it's no big deal.

There's nothing to show

prodding won't heal.

Try

If I stand up and face my fear

what will happen to me here?

On this earth, I'm not quite brave

even though I try and try.

If there is anything to be saved

then I will gladly help.

But where do I find my courage?

How can I?

The Progression Of Friendship

Day one

'Hey, how are you?'

I'm well, and you?

'Doing just fine, thanks. I'll catch you later.'

Okay, see you!

Day two

'Hey, how's it going?'

Good! And you?

Day ten

'Hey there!'

Hey!

Day twenty

'Hi.'

Hey!

Day thirty

'Sorry we haven't hung out in a while,

been busy with some stuff, catch you later?'

Sure, why not? No worries.

Day forty

'Gosh hi, I've been meaning to call you,

just so busy with work! How about this weekend?'

I can't this weekend, sorry.

Day eighty

'Hey, I know it's been a while, we've both been pretty busy, haven't we? How about we do something this week? Miss hanging out with you.'

I would really love that. I've been needing someone to talk to lately.

Day one hundred

'Sorry I couldn't make it the last few weeks,

Things got pretty hectic for me.

Hope you're doing well and let's plan for some time soon.'

Yeah, it's whatever, it's fine. I haven't been

doing so great either.

I could really use someone to vent to.

Day 130

'Hey, hi, hello! Sorry again, it's been awhile!'

...

Day 135

...

...

Day 150

...

...

Day 185

I really needed you,

and you were always lost in your own ambitions.

I really needed you,

and you couldn't care to say the least.

I really needed you,

and your ego was in the way.

I really needed you,

and nothing I said made you realize and stay.

You were a shitty friend, and I should never have stuck around

as long as I had.

I really needed you,

and I sound petty for saying all of this.

But I really needed you,

and now I'm finally able to say

All I really needed was for you to keep asking

that same question that you asked so little of the time.

All I really needed,

was for you to ask those three words,

That one simple question.

"How are you?"

I really needed you, you really needed me to, but as life tends to go

To and fro,

We get sidetracked and sidestepped and we each drift to somewhere that seems so much more important at the time.

In our human experience, we all need each other.

Day 200

"Hey. How are you?"

Not good. You?

"Same. Want to talk about it?"

Sure.

Flaws

We all have flaws

there is no perfect diagram

being bound by all these laws

makes it difficult to know who I really am.

Shall I say, 'go ahead'

and deny my pencil full of lead?

Keep on walking here and straight

not daring to test the line?

Stop at a closed gate

and don't dare search for a sign?

I think I'll take my chances

flaws or not I'll make due

for as a multitude dances

I might stumble in my steps

maybe bumping into you.

White Clouds

                    Looked up at the sky today

    wondering what's to come

   not sure if there are any clouds

doesn't the sky usually have some?

                     Don't you see the shroud?

     Covering up the sun

     the dark veils of rain

      everything gray,

not knowing what's there to gain.

    If it were to storm

no planted seeds would grow.

    If it were to drizzle

There just might be a chance.

                Let the wind howl and blow

Leave The Dreaming To The Flowers - Tiffiny Rose Allen

let the trees sway

for here is where I'll stay.

Here is where I'm strong

      for I know the dark clouds will pass

the showers will dry

white clouds will return so very fast.

Seeds will have grown

and all will be well.

          Yes, all will be well.

Time

There were times when I thought I'd fail

and there were times when I failed.

Things used to be such wonder

never knowing where to travel

only asking for the future

ever so kindly to unravel.

Then the sky turned to gray

And the future looked at me.

It said

"It appears to be,

a trouble has come,

one not easily discarded

for certain things have you not regarded."

Leave The Dreaming To The Flowers - Tiffiny Rose Allen

So here I am now,

right here

Smiles covering a frown

Laughing though I want to cry.

A test of fate

a shed of hate

only begging, only praying

for time to be kind.

Here

Too many days have I sat alone

too many days have I not seen the sun.

You could cry yourself to sleep

you could cry yourself to death.

You can laugh at your pride and stand at my side

or you could run away and be a shame

out before it's time to seek your fame.

I've listened to your faults

locked your secrets away in vaults.

No one will sneak inside

no one will wander.

Just hold my hand, sit beside me

don't stray, just guide me.

I'll follow you

If you follow me

maybe we'll be

something heroic

something grand

or maybe we'll just be here

In this place.

Here in this memory

In this song

In this verse.

Maybe we'll just be here

just right here.

Earth Remains

Say hello to the morning

oh, wait, it's now afternoon.

Waiting for the stars to shine

but the sun is still so high.

My thoughts are in a scramble

what seems blue turns out to be green.

My eyes do long for sleep

yet my mind urges me to remain aware.

Life is no easy thing

It changes every day.

But one thing we will always have

is the beauty of this earth.

The sunset will always remain

a trance, a portrait, a moment.

It will always be vital

to our every deed.

For the simple beauty of grandeur

the glorious beauty of this world

is something we all need.

A Storm

I am but a hidden shadow

I am but an open flower.

Sitting in the rain

staring at the storm clouds

watching everything come down

'til water rushes toward me.

Beginning to run

beginning to scream

climb up the tree

hold on tight to the branches

whispering, whispering

eyes closed, whispering

'I am but a hidden shadow

I am but an open flower.'

Whispering, whispering

open those eyes

all was a dream.

Letting Go And Walking Forward

Look up at the sky

see it's gorgeous blue forever

so old and so clear

so blue, so white its clouds.

If that goes on forever,

what else could?

If that goes on forever,

what else could?

Is it harmony, is it love?

A warm hand to hold

a kiss to blow

a flower to pick

a smile to give?

Is that what we call happiness?

Can you recall the happy times?

The times that stand so near but that you cannot relive.

All that is now is present

past and future still exist

what matters, still exists.

Life will go on

but will you go on with it

or just stand by

and let it fade away?

It comes it goes

But you can only catch it once

You can only have it then.

You can't hold onto it for a rainy day

you can't put it in a box and leave it be.

Life has breath

breath has words

words have song

and they find where they belong.

~

We are not friends anymore,

and I do not say that with a negative tone

For we are truly different people now.

I just want to say

thank you for the things you've shown me,

for the things I was able to show you.

For without them

we would not be

who we have made ourselves to be.

Leave The Dreaming To The Flowers - Tiffiny Rose Allen

Part III

~Author's Note~

The poems in this section suggest the happenings of coming in to one's self. Figuring out your own relationship to faith, to God, seeing hypocrisy in its wake and starting to speak up, taking the pain that surrounds you and seeking the good that is strewn into the air.

Containing

Dreams Mixed Into Life **93**

Nobility **95**

Sunsets **97**

Jealousy **100**

Hold Faith **103**

Now And Again **105**

Sowing Life **108**

A Book Does Beckon **110**

Birdsong **112**

Cast A Spell **114**

Heroic Story **116**

Progression **118**

Age **121**

Stars **122**

Leave The Dreaming To The Flowers - Tiffiny Rose Allen

~

Funny how things inspire

how they become things we admire.

Things we exalt and cheer for

sometimes even shed a tear for.

Be that which we aspire

Be that which we admire

Sometimes leads to a dire matter.

Inspiration lies in the wind

it blows all around.

Through the trees and under rivers

That which gives us shivers

In the cold of night

In the cool of shade.

'Tis that which causes us to write.

~

Dreams Mixed Into Life

Days turn up and days turn down

things not all can decide,

we could never know how

our lives play out.

So before you wipe away your smile

and turn it to a frown,

check your dreams and hold them tight

keep them all year round.

Don't know how we've managed

sometimes it's like a blur

life can be so very dull

when we don't know for sure

I have lived a thousand years

seen so much joy and pain.

Leave The Dreaming To The Flowers - Tiffiny Rose Allen

To look up at the sky

to gaze up at the stars

to notice your place in this universe

and not let your heart go down

Even when you drift through that course

the wind will bring you sound.

open your eyes and realize

that nightmares do disappear.

The sun will rise

when no one denies

that it's okay to wake up.

It's okay to wake up.

Nobility

I have heard Christians defy the works of their own God.

They say that witchcraft is evil, it is false

All other religions are false

Quite commonly, they use the word 'false'

They are not the only ones.

In every aspect in every place,

religion, spirituality, lifestyle, philosophy,

they will always try to prove the other wrong.

Only one way, one way,

time to ignore all the rest.

What is not realized is,

the power of prayer is in itself an energy source.

Vibrations, thoughts, dynamism, karma,

What goes out in the world will come back around.

Perhaps it is

Not willing, not wanting,

but just a factor of the life we live.

Do not disprove what is unknown to you

unless it becomes known.

Thoughts and opinions,

sure, let them be.

Just give kindness all around because

we're all bound for the graveyard.

Sunsets

If I was a warrior

I don't know who I'd fight.

I'd probably just turn tables

and make a hideaway from sight.

If I was a ruler

don't know who I'd rule

I'd just be following

and looking to you.

There was a beginning

the start of a tale,

it told of sunsets learning to breathe.

I was so afraid

didn't know who I could trust

but in this crumbled cave

I saw a shadow of light.

There used to be a law

for anyone who dared to sing

if there were a simple melody

it would be stripped raw.

I caught a distraction

a turn of my eyes

It was a sunset that vanquished all lies.

If you knew something

a secret to be kept

I wouldn't trouble you

For a sealed tongue is rare.

We all make promises

That mostly aren't kept

We pray for the dark

when the sun hasn't left.

I caught a sunset

I held it to my heart

it has kept me warm

on these cold frigid nights.

I do love the stars

The moon and the dark,

I do love the sound

when the earth is coated in the night.

Jealousy

Gazing towards the earth,

grass over dark dirt,

thoughts floating in an abyss,

candlewax dripping on the candlestick.

Eyes as they dwell

in the past, the future

past, future.

We may never be everything we desire

we may grow jealous and weary

day in, day out.

We will be jealous of others

others will be jealous of us

and yet there is supposed to be no room for envy in our hearts,

they say.

We try to push away the sin

Even though it merely wraps itself around our flesh.

It's an ocean that we constantly drown in

tortured and marred

It's an evil tune that lures us to our downfall.

A seductive whisper that bleeds poison,

human nature, pushed towards this.

No one is focusing on what's right.

It is not what you do

not how you do it,

but who's there with you

through it all.

Nothing matters,

apart from love.

Hold Faith

Sunlight and stopping rays

come in, go out

are the ways.

We count on one

there goes another

hold tight to faith

but do not smother.

Overwhelm, will come contempt

hopelessness and corruption become unveiled.

Reclaim.

Not a false attempt,

fear is when a face is paled.

Do not lose,

oh dear, do not lose

always hold on to something.

For if there is no rope

when you enter the deep sea

indeed

you will

become lost.

Now And Again

As each moment passes

my thoughts become words.

They get written out

pen and ink

become separate from my mind

so if forgotten it is no loss.

As each star shines

I look at the sky

knowing the sun will hide them soon.

Yet I cannot take in all their present beauty.

I may for granted take tomorrow

and the day after too

and every second I cannot promise a magnificent life.

The clock will tick and tick on still

my heart will beat until the last drop,

and right now, I am happy

right now, the stars do smile

right now, I am writing

Right now, is all I've got—

because tomorrow doesn't exist yet.

~

Kneading away,

a cat wants affection

black lightbulb

light in the room but still so dark.

Dark fantasy plays on the TV,

sleep setting in,

not just yet.

Sowing Life

Mood swing, frustration

mind rift, manipulation.

Jump out of it then back you go

something so simple, turned low.

Progress, protection's feat is

scrambling for a bit of meat.

Priorities are expired,

those that were admired

grew old and out of tune,

everyone has left

and now you're staring at the moon.

Cars drive by, and the sun sets,

it is not about what everybody gets

It is what everybody sows,

no one has gone in rows,

Leave The Dreaming To The Flowers - Tiffany Rose Allen

no one is aware of what they know.

A Book Does Beckon

The chronic sounds from a cricket

murmurs through the walls

I can hear my steady breathing

and the writing of this pen.

The sound of skin brushing against paper

Tv is talking to my door

whispers about unknown persons

coffee pouring in the air.

A book is on my mind,

but the crickets won't let me read

the book is on my nightstand

but the hour is too dark.

Everything in the world is telling me naught

my eyes even betray me.

The soul's thirst for fiction's tea is too enticing

no manner can stop that deep craving.

Birdsong

Day upon day

all there is, is rain.

Pouring, storming,

no intermission

and among all the rain

I could still hear the birds sing

when day began to break.

Here I am faced with chaos,

I don't shed any tears now.

I don't worry now.

I am not afraid now.

The sun shines its brightest

when the clouds depart

and the birdsong encourages,

causing the sun to see the earth.

Cast A Spell

I'll cast a spell

so that I can tell

if the world suits me.

I'll look all around

And see the profound reality.

Touch the wind and kiss it goodbye

run from the rain and don't cry.

Grab a shield and protect your pain.

Forget the walls for just a day

Listen to the stars, and how they decay,

this moment and forever.

We'll see the world through a fever

it'll pass, and it'll grow

and it will be then that we know

what we decided for the future.

Heroic Story

Calm,

we're at ease

let down the barriers

welcome the foreign breeze.

My steps, they will waver

my heart, it will skip

a gift is what they gave her

but the wrapping isn't what caused her to slip.

Trusting the wrong world

destruction became unfurled

the bottle did tip

but not the ordinary poison.

She dreamt of love and a blue sky

and turned the wrong into a right.

Life returned, and we all lived.

Predictable story,

possibly,

But sometimes predictable is still extraordinary.

Progression

Mess is all around

we're not thinking straight

kindness is too bound

I hope it's not too late.

Walked the lonely road

taught me how to be

there is nothing better

than knowing you're happy.

That brightness in your eyes

it's blinding me from afar

with you there's no place for lies

we'll heal that old scar.

Look up at the night

see the stars ever bright

they reflect your eyes

you make the moon despise.

Take ahold of my hand

I'm holding on, to you

together we will stand

together we'll be true.

Truth is hard to know

don't play this for show

I tried to make the right call

but you stood on it all.

I won't shatter my bones

I won't strengthen my tears

the glory you're shown

will fade through the years.

Leave The Dreaming To The Flowers - Tiffiny Rose Allen

I'm closing my eyes

no sight upon you.

When the sun rises,

I'll start again, new.

Age

Don't you worry about getting old,

don't you worry about the future too much.

It is not good for you

worry is never good.

So much life lies in front of you

chase that

don't chase shadows

shadows are not vital

perhaps they are destined to taunt and

anticipate your mood

But you've got so much more than a shadowed mind.

You've got so much to look forward to.

Stars

The stars swim around me

an island of galaxies

drowning me in dreams.

My head caught in the sky

So hard to come back down each time I try.

The fantasies comfort me more than here

I walk, each time holding back a tear.

Make me fly,

let me swim in the milky way

right now, today.

I know, I must wait.

I've so much life

So much I must give

I have so much I feel ready to burst.

Leave The Dreaming To The Flowers - Tiffiny Rose Allen

I'll wait, oh patiently I'll wait.

A strain, a pull, each day I will tread

on and on

without fraud.

The galaxies must wait

wait a long, long while

and that's okay, for I've lots to do

my daydreams will give me something to look forward too.

Through all the mischiefs

and snares I encounter along the way

the stars will be there.

~

Don't give up too soon

we've still so far to go.

Dear, don't give me up.

Leave The Dreaming To The Flowers - Tiffiny Rose Allen

Part IV

~Author's Note~

Dealing with other people's opinions and projections of us when we have so much to deal with within ourselves and our lives, is truly extraordinary when we think about it. The poems in this section focus on a juggle of explanation or simply moving on, opening our hearts to love after they've been trampled on. Somehow always finding a way back to ourselves.

Containing

Across The Desert **128**

Humanity's Bribe **130**

Problems **132**

Not A Simple Time **134**

Mirage **136**

Chance **138**

Future Plans **139**

Time's Burden **140**

Not In Vain **141**

Thanks For The Temporary Company (Part I) **143**

Thanks For The Temporary Company (Part II) **148**

Soliloquy **152**

See The Light **153**

Voyage **156**

Final Breath **159**

Battle **160**

Love's Kiss **161**

Delusional Hope **162**

Leave The Dreaming To The Flowers - Tiffiny Rose Allen

Across The Desert

Pockets full of smoke.

Dashes are in the dirt.

Flowers are in my mind

 Weeds are in my hair.

When I awoke

the wind was a desert

my eyes were sand,

and my feet were thorns.

Step each step

got farther away

the rain was ice

mud was snow,

the journey wouldn't end

wouldn't let me pretend.

No farce allowed

no tea to sip

only to move farther

step after step.

Shortcut swiped

Legs are hard to move

 but still I must walk on.

I won't give in

the desert won't have me

I won't give in

No matter how hard it grabs me.

Humanity's Bribe

Finding the heart

looking the part.

Searching my way

almost getting there

something made me stay.

To go now

I don't know where

A half has been snapped

the ordeal constantly recapped.

So hard to shut them out

oh God, I want to shout.

The walls of a shelter

stripped away, a departure.

Life turned a path

It's more complicated than math.

Please clear your head

I can't believe these things you've said.

Hope got slapped

faith got trapped

fate got remapped.

And still, I am here.

Living frightened like a little deer

and still, I tread on,

not accepting humanity's bribe.

Problems

Will the world run away?

Is a song better unsung?

I may not know the way

I may do something that's better undone,

all drawn out and gone to run.

How will I survive under this sun?

Question,

go on,

ask me a question.

Nearer,

come on,

are we getting nearer?

Hard to stand tall, hard to scream

It's just nothing doesn't it seem?

Leave The Dreaming To The Flowers - Tiffiny Rose Allen

It's all too large, and it's punched too small.

I will try to knock down the wall.

Will we sit here

will we rise?

I'm just left here,

Swimming in lies.

See me,

know me,

you will find

that it was a hard bind.

Not A Simple Time

I can't control your fate

I can't choose what you will and will not do.

I can't be prepared when the lightning strikes

for I won't know the precise moment it happens.

The boat won't sail

on fallen tears

the sun won't rise

on a discouraged heart.

It won't stop me from being sad.

I will sit alone in the darkness

if that will ease the pain.

Futures put into play

'I'm sorry'

will not bring a change

Has a life been spoiled,

have cities been burned,

and have people been hung

All by innocuous words?

Mirage

Only for you

will I stand strong against this wall.

It pushes me to my core

Yet to waver I will not.

Rain falls in my eyes

Masks my tears of strain

a mirage is in the distance

I fall into its rapture for a moment

and each time it gets harder and harder

to pull myself back.

Yet I do

this time and next time.

I'll turn back to stone

and the process will be replayed.

But not forever.

Never forever.

Only a while

that will one day seem like mere minutes.

~

I hold to you for so long

my heart doesn't falter

which in a way worries me

my heart should beat, I should breathe.

Yet there is no drumbeat to be heard.

Chance

I saw the speeding light

and I took the road by night.

We had to run but were not quick

we had to go but could not pick.

The time was fast, yet it felt so slow

we flew so high but felt so low.

Took a chance and it got us here

right now, I don't think it's too wrong of a steer.

Let this just be and we will see

how tomorrow comes.

Future Plans

Remind me of my path

cause the road is getting hard to see.

A smoke is surfacing

starting to choke.

No matter how I seem

It's all cloudy like a dream.

The smoke got in my head

it's weighing down on me

all these words I've said

make my heart beat too slow.

I must take a breath

my heart just stopped right in my chest.

Time's Burden

They think it's okay

they think it's okay

to take us away and make us feel worn.

A lifetime can happen within a single day.

An hour or so can make me age a thousand years.

And the days will thrive, and I will survive

no matter how known my soul.

Not In Vain

I've been searching for the sun

I've been searching for a sign.

They smile like they've won

Eyes glaring with a demeaning shine.

All seems hopeless, all seems lost

I'm wandering, stuck in my thoughts.

It's got to be a maze

it's got to be a puzzle.

We must move the clouds and get out of this dark haze.

I'll get a pick; I'll get a chisel

whatever it takes, but no dismissal.

Feel a drop of rain

It's going to start a storm.

It won't be in vain.

~

Try to solve the day

get through it, you will see

that the puzzle will slowly fade away

and finally, we will finally

just know how to be.

Thanks For The Temporary Company

(Part I)

You're going to make a call

you're going to stand so tall

you're going to show them all—

Maybe we weren't made to be aristocrats

maybe we were born to dwell along with all the rats.

Oh,

I always preferred animals to people anyway,

big getups to pass the time

no,

I'd rather have the choice

to sit alone or rejoice.

Leave The Dreaming To The Flowers - Tiffiny Rose Allen

I'm not going to face the crowd

I'd rather hide in my shroud of comfort.

Come on now,

play a beat for me,

show me

how it's going to be

'cause I'm done.

I don't really know how

we can all still manage to bow.

I thought your knees were weak

I thought you forgot how to speak.

No wonder's trial

no wonder's trial.

I'm bored.

Too busy to be ignored

when I'm free you cut right through the cord.

Leave The Dreaming To The Flowers - Tiffiny Rose Allen

Oh, I'm bored.

I'm not going to deal with this bell

it is too loud for me,

stop ringing and let go.

You dress in ball gowns

and strut around

and we're lying here

and we're dying dear

and no one stops to see if you're okay.

How are you going to deal, anyway?

Pick up and change your course

no one will hear that voice so hoarse.

But you licked the roof anyway,

you said you'd stay,

and you left.

Funny how that is.

Go and play in your masquerades

hide your face and don't show any of your youth

lovely, you're buying out the truth.

Forget those bags,

I'd rather you dressed up in rags,

cause then I'd know you're honest,

then I'd know you're kind,

but when the world's upon us

and with the ropes, they bind,

I'm not going to be okay

so you can go ahead and walk away.

I'll just be right here

and I'll do my best to get rid of my fear—

Thanks for the temporary company.

Thanks For The Temporary Company
(Part II)

I want you to know that I'm okay

feelings just got me down.

They don't know

what I don't say —

you know that trouble is in a mound.

Sorrow came to find me—

it knocked on heaven's gate.

Maybe it didn't understand the curfew

because it would've known it was too late.

Honey, come and find me,

sing me softly, to sleep.

Find me in emotion

know that I'm yours to keep.

Sorrow came to find me

It knocked on heaven's gate.

I told it to leave

but it wouldn't retrieve,

so I made the mistake

of opening the gate.

Sorrow made an observation

it came close to my ear,

it said "Honey, what's in your pocket?

Baby, why don't you come near?"

I tried to find a legion,

for the angels all flew away

sorrow said, "I am one, and with life comes decay."

Forget the unsaid verses

forget the unthought plans.

Maybe we were only meant for curses,

I still want to go and feel the sands.

I want you to know that I'm okay,

feelings just got me down,

they don't know

what I don't say,

you know that trouble is in a mound.

Fight my freedom, come kingdom

that light ain't fading away,

reflection's just a deep end

plummet without delay.

Swim your victory to the top

don't let sorrow stand in your way.

Fight my freedom, come kingdom.

Know that I'm okay.

Soliloquy

I don't know the time

dreams are calling out to me

the pen still writes fast,

even though my mind wants to sleep.

I had something priceless

something that was mine

it was torn away

and I've had to deal with it every day.

Pages are yellow; ink is blue

music turned to lullaby

eyes are stubborn too.

People smother so, and there's nothing to do.

See The Light

Can you see some joy in the air?

It was placed there for someone

it is perceived as beauty and taken for granted,

only the patient can really see.

You can make it yours if you like,

gather the colors and hold them to your chest,

you're not low

you're humble

and you're free.

Now,

When the earth is coated in the night,

you'll be able to look inside yourself

and see the light.

Leave The Dreaming To The Flowers - Tiffiny Rose Allen

Leave The Dreaming To The Flowers - Tiffiny Rose Allen

Leave The Dreaming To The Flowers - Tiffiny Rose Allen

Voyage

Looked up, eyes stuck to the skies

stardust falling into my eyes

blinked tears that turned to gold

rolling down my cheeks

falling to earth so cold.

Stepped into the sea

iced mists float above

peered at all the sorrow

saw what I was among.

Further, I walked, rising

over my head they were,

the waves crashing when I gazed among the pure.

Covered in the way

no reason to delay

on I walked

feet touching a floor of sand.

The creatures in my path

Did try to mislead

told me things I couldn't answer

my thoughts unable to form a sentence.

When I placed my steps upon a new shore

Having traveled through an ocean's core

I did take a deep breath of air

then laid down my head.

Eyes facing up to the skies again

Stars made into constellations tell me a story.

I'll hear it 'til the sun makes it fade,

then I'll rise

and find it again.

Final Breath

Disguising insolence and making love to the ungodly,

we journey so,

throughout the time of our body.

When our hands are worn

And we're laid down to rest

there's no doubt in my mind

that indeed we still live.

We grow our wings and begin to fly

some people think it's a shame to die.

It is of course

but only if we lacked the life we lived.

Battle

Saw the horizon

I made a mistake.

Gave away my armor

the arrows did fly.

Stood in the open air

and indeed, I was struck.

Wounds that will heal

no need to cry

tomorrow will come

and we're halfway there.

Dry your eyes

we're on a journey.

The destination is not too far

we're in this together.

Love's Kiss

Light of my being

joy of my soul

I'll love you more than you'll ever know.

I'll love you still

when the sun eats the sky

when the birds cease to fly

when my heart has stopped beating

and I beg for a breath

I'll love you still

even upon death.

Delusional Hope

What is this?

A drop of hope or just a dream?

Is it too big for reality?

A flower seed not yet grown,

immature energy stirred

I surely wish not,

for excitement is a wish

a burning of such warmth

kept close to the heart.

A spark in the eye,

a smile upon a face

teeth to gleam

Oh, what grace

hopeful delusion has already begun

just as the leaves fall.

Leave The Dreaming To The Flowers - Tiffiny Rose Allen

Part V

~Author's Note~

The poems in this section give a focus on acceptance, a focus on longing, wishing that certain things were different but accepting them for what they are. Human emotion at its core, the hope of walking forward, no matter if it is alone or with another.

Containing

Life **166**

First Impressions **168**

Over A Book **169**

17 **170**

Simple Things, They Matter **171**

Check Your Clock **173**

Rain Thoughts **175**

The Game **177**

One Of Us Is Truth **179**

What Could I Believe? **181**

Night Wishes **183**

What Am *I* Afraid To Be? **185**

Choices **188**

Praying For Your Time **190**

His Smile **191**

Pavement **194**

Letter **196**

Life

I have some scars, who doesn't?

We look at the table and judge the people sitting in it

we ignore that we all eat from the same plate.

We're all in the same pen.

I used to be so afraid of sin,

but when you realize that it's all around you

I guess you just learn to walk through.

On and on the journey takes you

farther out into a desert

naturally you have no resources

but that's okay

because you've accepted yourself.

And in a sense, you are free.

And because you are free

You've grown wings to fly into the clouds

you'll drink the rain and sleep on soft satin

and find the beauty in everything.

First Impressions

Thinking of the spring

help me get there soon

make a tune come true,

my heart's role was not rehearsed

so I'm left just improvising

and stumbling as I speak.

I'm shy, I'm red, I'm weak.

Your voice does amplify

Sweet music to my ears,

oh, I can't count my fears.

Yet here I sit and wait for you

Acquaintance or not

you've left an impression on me

and I can't shake it off.

Over A Book

Hand me a book

I will take a look

see the words you've seen

react differently and the same.

A page can reveal, and a page can disclose

that book there, hiding your nose.

Security measure, space bar

I like it all the same.

So long as we can talk

I'll like it all the same.

17

Hello, seventeen. Be kind to me alright?

Thirteen led to new beginnings

fourteen led to friendship

fifteen led to falling outs

and sixteen led to adventures

with some stress thrown in too.

I am a very lucky girl

though I have a lot on my plate.

My life is not an envious one

though social media might imply.

I am so grateful for all that I have been given

and all that I have done.

I did my best to make that year a good one.

Simple Things, They Matter

Been looking at the flowers today

and I think oh how I don't want any good thing to fade.

Run my hands through the water

and then it makes me wonder

what am I going to do?

Keep trudging through the darkness

It's alright, it's almost clear.

Everything isn't so bad

I've got much yet to do.

Sit and see it over

look up and smile at the moon.

Simple things, they matter

nothing is for sure.

You, you make me smile

don't go away too soon.

All my friends they leave me,

I walk often all alone.

Yet that's okay 'cause maybe,

I wouldn't have noticed you at all.

Check Your Clock

What is limitless, what is frail?

Is it a flower petal, suspension in air?

Or is it a feeling of being embraced?

No shadow can hold where there is love to unfold.

Though every stream and every force may try to consume

whatever drop of untouchable light is there

only the two who first started out

who first had eyes, can take hold the other's hand

and walk-through oblivion.

One must believe, and one must know,

no matter where time leads, you may forego,

you may step forward.

Only silence is the curse

only silence can stop this verse.

Sonder is mind consuming,

take hold of my hand and close your eyes.

Let's not think of all the people who will only despise.

Each individuality covered in envy

no time for that, now

no time.

Time is the only thing that brings the world closer,

but we've all got other things on our minds.

Rain Thoughts

Rain falls down and hits the trees,

wasn't long until I thought of you.

Wind does blow, but a simple breeze

wasn't long until I thought of you.

Hide a spell and maker's pain

fog had covered the wings that flew

wasn't long until I thought of you.

Not of past or trouble's bane,

not of melancholy despair,

a longing that was new

wasn't long until I thought of you.

Leave The Dreaming To The Flowers - Tiffiny Rose Allen

A kiss of hand that may must wait,

smile silly at your word,

no matter if it were to be late

perhaps the time will be cured.

I don't wish to purge of this mood anew,

wasn't long until I thought of you.

The Game

Should've seen my sorrow,

told me where to go.

The stars don't know where to find me

I'm so used to the run and hide.

Sitting still doesn't calm me

It makes me want to scream.

Sometimes I need to halt

and breathe in the air.

Sometimes I need to run and see what's out there for me.

It's hard to tell when to tell, what to tell, how.

It's hard to live a game,

but everyone knows the game of life,

everyone knows there are no winners.

Such a pessimistic view,

Leave The Dreaming To The Flowers - Tiffiny Rose Allen

I'd like to plant a flower

so that something good can come from the bad

not bowing to this power.

One Of Us Is Truth

You tell me I can't fight the stars

to let be what will be

perhaps I don't want to settle for what's supposed to be.

I want to be out there,

breathing in the air

not settling for a damaged life.

I am not what happened in the past; the past let be,

I am not what the past does break

we all learn from every mistake,

and if I'm to back down and let the previous walk all over me

well, I guess I won't be sorry to say fuck you eternally.

Leave The Dreaming To The Flowers - Tiffiny Rose Allen

The past is not set in stone;

every person has a separate definition of what was.

I have mine, and you have yours,

one of us is truth, one of us is truth.

I'm not letting the memories take me away,

not this time.

I have a future to uphold.

What Could I Believe?

Can we wake up for tomorrow?

Can we play another note?

Could we tell secrets to the stars

and ignore the talk of man?

Perhaps I could find my courage

and say what's on my mind,

silly girl like me,

what could I believe?

What could I believe?

I could believe that we are not lost

we are not wandering,

we are whatever we can be

in this bewildered reality.

Isn't that enough?

I'm to go out and live, but what if there is no company?

Well then, that will just have to be.

Night Wishes

My mind is fooling me tonight,

my thoughts are heavy and full of worry, again.

Yet somehow in a second,

they fade away.

I want to close my eyes and dream of you.

I want to see the everything you do.

All that is you,

all that is you.

I want to feel your hand on my cheek

hear you smile, hear you laugh.

No static, no muffle, clear

and right here.

To tease me,

to hold me.

I want to hold you.

I want to wipe your demons to the bottom of the earth

And I want to gaze into your eyes,

And see them glow.

What Am *I* Afraid To Be?

What am *I* afraid to be?

What am *I* afraid to be?

Afraid to be loud,

afraid to be quiet,

too clingy or not attached enough

I am afraid to be an adult

thrown into a forced reality.

Afraid to be a burden

afraid to be a girl

I am afraid to be a leader

for I am not sure of the right way,

and I am afraid to be a follower

for I don't know who to follow.

I contradict myself, I know

every word I say battles the other,

just as my life

just as my mind.

Consistently fighting myself and not paying attention

to the fact that I am loved.

That I am allowed to be loved.

Some days it's all fine, and I run around carefree

other days my mind decides to replay some memories.

I am afraid to be okay

because the good things don't often last.

I have accepted that phrase,

and what I must remind myself in spite of my mind

and this world,

is that good things do come

and if you respect them and give them the proper care

they just might hold on.

Choices

They say that we don't choose our family

but we can choose our friends

I disagree with that claim entirely

I actually think that it is the other way around

You don't choose who you love

you don't choose who you bond with.

Just because one is related to you by blood,

does not mean that they are your family.

We do not choose who walks in and out of our lives,

we do not choose who stays.

Sometimes the person you love the most fades from you

and no matter what you do or what you say

there is no stop to it.

Sometimes it's easier to tell a stranger your deepest thought,

they won't tell anyone you know, for they don't know you,

they don't know who your ties are with.

The world is complex,

but if you don't strain your eyes when you look at it,

you'll see how simple it is.

Praying For Your Time

Are you with me, or are you gone?

I've been praying for your time.

I've been praying for your time.

Listen to me, don't go quickly,

hold my hand and talk to me.

Hold me baby, hold me close,

It's okay to feel this ponder and morose.

Love me slowly but with soul

and don't let our lives grow dull.

To be with you is grace

a fragrance yet unknown

but sweetest as could taste

will someday hopefully be shown.

His Smile

His smile is small, and not as grand as it used to be.

He used to smile, all the time, just for me.

His smiles were just for me.

No one could ever make me laugh just quite the same as him.

Oh, his smile was small, and now it is not as grand as it used to be.

Only a moment, he was mine.

Knives slashed and tried to cut our strings

I can't find him anymore.

I scream, and I scream, but I do not think that he hears me.

My love, you were my only paradise in a swimming chaotic space.

Constellations tried to drown me;

galaxies got too close.

My universe was only you.

Leave The Dreaming To The Flowers - Tiffiny Rose Allen

No matter how far,

You were always right here,

now I don't know where you've gone.

His smile is small, and not as grand as it used to be.

I wonder if he'll maybe, someday, again smile for me.

If not, I'll take my steps; I will heal.

The journey will not be an easy one

for I am used to having his shoulder to lean on.

I want to know why he has stopped smiling

I want to help this boy I love.

Yet I don't know if he can hear me.

Can he hear through this flesh and skull?

My thoughts and my unspoken words.

The tears that I cried

can he hear them?

My smile is small, and not as grand as it used to be.

Perhaps it is because I am now so unaware

of what lays here for me.

Pavement

I feel like an extra stone

on a pavement made of marble.

All the steps are flow and smooth

while I jut out and protrude.

Wind blows over me

not taking mind,

I hope the breeze rounds my edges

So that I can feel like everyone else again.

Standing in the center

Whilst drifted off

mind to another sphere

what is happening here?

All the marble soft and sleek

oh, the soft words they speak.

Hand in the water

wanting to dip lower

submerge in a different dimension.

Far away from the whispers

Far away from the façade.

It is savagely sweet.

Steps along the marble,

solid and secure

I jut out and protrude

Oh, how could I allude

The steps that walk past

paying no mind.

Letter

Eyes are closed

wind is blown

heart beat faster

thoughts a riot

Flower in hand

petals are soft

don't want to drop it

don't want to share.

A letter from far away

and I'm lost

thoughts and thoughts and thoughts.

I don't want to stay.

~

Some things are good forever,

some things not so much.

Some things are only passing,

we should embrace it all the same.

Today is mine forever, even if it is only fleeting.

I'll make memories by passing by another,

Even if it's just hello.

Part VI

~Author's Note~

We can be kind whilst standing up for ourselves. We can throw around kindness like confetti and still know when to say that we deserve more, that we are allowed to think differently, and that we are allowed to hold onto hope in trying times.

Containing

Masquerade **200**

I Ain't The People **202**

Four Letter Word **204**

Neon Whore **208**

Metal Bird **211**

Matter **212**

Misused Social Words **217**

Thinking Of **219**

Carpe Diem **222**

Smile **224**

Words For What Is **226**

Street Love **228**

Stardust Afternoon **230**

Earth Child **231**

Masquerade

Put a smile on your mask

go on,

make it bright

don't let anyone know you're not alright.

We're going to a ball,

a masquerade of facts,

fibs, and lies, and war.

That is how we are joined

That is how we are upheld.

Do you have this all down?

Pay attention now,

take in the scene,

smoky masks all around

all eyes are turned

dresses are spinning

your heart is spinning

the world is spinning

fall down.

Don't fall down,

dance in your gown

hold up your mask.

And here, we fool.

I Ain't The People

I ain't the people and the people ain't me.

Climb too far to hit unruly.

There you are,

hating on my family

think you're better,

think you're bad.

You should be glad I'm not ripping you to shreds.

Fuck your worth.

Fuck your scowl.

You don't know what I'm going to do.

I'm through.

I'm through.

You're not for me,

you're not my family.

You're just a shadow

that will hate on continually.

I ain't the people, and the people ain't me,

Ha, you're funny.

"Peace, peace, but there is no peace"

Said Jeremiah.

Your face is smiling, but you're lying,

I can tell.

You want 'peace, peace, but there is no peace,'

no contract, no lease.

No truce when it comes to the ones who matter.

'I'm wrong, you're wrong, no you.'

I ain't the people, and the people ain't me.

You should have chosen your words more carefully.

Four Letter Word

Wondering about that word

so short, so precious, and tossed around.

Not the word of love,

we all know about that one aplenty.

It is said sincerely,

then gets overwhelmed;

it is tossed and turned by the wrong ones

and the wrong ways.

Same goes for the other word.

Yet I do not think it is thought upon as much.

Seize the day

take that adventure

go do what makes your soul smile

Phrases and catchphrases

wound and rewound.

The word I am talking about is life.

So blatant and so subtle; life.

Upon our first breath

It begins and it ends and we suffer and we laugh.

It is a paradox, it is complex, it is strong, and it is weak

as we toss around words of living, as others are dying and we are right behind but we don't care because we are living.

Or we just think that we're living.

That word constantly showing on media pages and motivations,

It is there,

it is there.

We see it and we read it

and we think on it and then we move on.

The start and the end.

Leave The Dreaming To The Flowers - Tiffiny Rose Allen

Time folds over itself as we drift in perpetual fatigue of overuse of the most precious thing we have and take for granted,

day upon day, upon sunrise, upon sunset

We take it and we think it is ours,

but it never belonged to us.

It does not belong to us.

It is a loan that is taken back indefinitely,

It is not yours; it is a temporary offering.

Treat it well and keep it in excellent condition,

because it goes back to the manufacturer once it's time.

Yet we never listen

and we come back,

bloodied and swollen and beaten up by the very thing

that is being returned.

A paradox, a labyrinth...

The hauntingly beautiful thing that is life.

Neon Whore

Angel's dancing and an evil concubine

neon whore was her name and she passed the time.

She broke free of her chained curtains

and rejoiced in lullaby

the silver astral cord

gave in to her design.

Neon whore,

out the door,

she wanted a reason to beat them at life

no use but worth a try

her sweet, sweet lullaby

brought the angels to rest.

Scissors cutting at the core,

she began to walk down from the sky

closer to earth and resting on a cloud

when the great storm began.

Clouds disappeared when rain did sway

and off she fell down,

into the lake

wet and naked she stood up high

not gazing at the passersby,

for she took her hair and wrapped

her breasts, her hips, her thighs

and walked until she could walk no more,

closer and closer to the sun's door.

Heavenly rays

so familiar she cried

glad to be free to sing her lullaby.

Soul re-enlivened and new steps applied

she channeled her strength and said

a temporary farewell.

Time to be tested and sought for deceit,

her next steps were to get shoes for her feet.

Metal Bird

Metal bird, metal bird,

I fell to the floor.

There you stood, bright and perfect

Though you were broken inside.

I never loved you more as you took your pieces and tried to repair me,

but nothing can be repaired.

The only cure would be your company, don't you know?

Two pieces of broken machinery trying to fix each other.

The cure is your company,

two souls seen eye to eye

make a bond not able to fit chains

I love your broken pieces,

don't worry about them.

Matter

Happiness resides in the soul,

at times, it is on the surface, ready to laugh and share its open style.

Other times,

it hides in the heart

and almost feels like it is not welcome here anymore.

Blue icicles freeze it into the past and try to burn out its flame.

Even when that flame of joy is burnt out, the smoke still resides.

It always resides.

When the sky turns into a whirlwind

and our hope is swept across oceans,

we reside.

No amount of pain can shatter the strong galaxy

of mesmerizing courage

that only depends on you.

There is no such thing as a human

that doesn't matter.

Your hair, your eyes, your skin

It matters,

don't say it doesn't matter.

Your thoughts, your actions, those steps

they matter.

Every breath that is taken,

whether it be of evil countenance or holy,

it matters on this earth.

Like every tree,

And every amount of oxygen they produce

matters for every being's survival.

We must all protect each other in order to survive.

Not survive to beat an enemy,

survive to save the broken.

Any hand held, hug given, kiss received

it centers around the core of the earth.

Causes the crystals to gain their power,

the ghosts to stop haunting,

the demons to stop taunting,

the howling oblivion to stop calling,

Your smile and your crooked teeth and those scars

They don't give an unnecessary impact.

Holding open a door,

may have just given a shred of that pure burning flame

to someone who was lost.

I know it is hard to move when you're in that swarm of people.

Standing in the corner with a drink in hand,

hiding from the everybody's,

stay kind to them.

Even if you wish their existence weren't a valid one,

Teach them,

show them,

kindness and love,

is the only way this world can cope.

We all need each other

if we refuse to admit it,

we do need each other.

So take a deep breath

and be a supporter,

a listener, sympathizer, empathizer, encourager, wanderer—

just show kindness in this long-lasting world.

It does not have a cost,

it does not have a refund,

it is an everlasting show of love

for all who feel they are undeserving.

You will never be undeserving.

Misused Social Words

They say on social media,

(I'm sure you can name the like)

They say face to face as well,

"I can't wait to spend my life with you."

I find it an offensive phrase,

meaning moved in with or marriage,

commitment of a long-term.

Fine as that may be,

that phrase in its entirety,

is degrading of the present state to me.

You are already living together side by side,

you are already spending your life together,

just in a different sense.

Leave The Dreaming To The Flowers - Tiffiny Rose Allen

Do not lose sight of what is already born and brought to life,

do not keep wishing for a more abundant future

if you are not even aware of your present.

You're together on a different path,

confiding, laughing, and leaning on.

Everyone wants more and more

forgetting what it is to already have.

You post on social media,

saying you're wanting more.

Look around you and receive,

you have what you're meant for now

it'll grow grander and you'll get married or moved in,

commitment of a long-term.

Just grow slowly, for patience is a virtue, after all.

Thinking Of

Laying here and looking up

Seeing that you're gone.

The fire's high and we're astray as we dream on.

Thinking of,

our part.

We need you and you need us

and we're already there.

The sun is high but we're still cold

and breathing in air.

Thinking of,

the past.

Beauty's gone and we're a mess

but we're still here.

We're fighting hard we're fighting strong

with every tear.

Love

is not gone.

Shaping up and carving past the last year's drought,

it wasn't bad it wasn't cruel

yet it had its blemish.

As we go on,

thinking of,

the present.

It's today and we're today and it's raining,

time to bring our jackets and raise our hoods and get through the clouds.

It's alright, and we're alright, as sun wades in,

shining down and beaming down against our skin.

Thinking of,

the future.

I'll wake up and look in those eyes,

Speechless, and taken, and smiling.

Thinking of,

Love.

So right now

I may not know

What's going to come.

We'll stick around and make a sound and start some trouble.

Guess it's now and we're okay and that's okay,

don't worry.

Carpe Diem

Look at the world,

perceive the sound,

what more could bear

the life in the air?

See at times it is good,

look up in glee,

passed all of the catastrophe.

Don't close those eyes

don't shut them tight

look through with your sight

see and make matter

the hours of stars.

Not astronomy, astrology, scientific, mathematic,

the lights in the sky and how you go on.

Leave The Dreaming To The Flowers - Tiffiny Rose Allen

Coming together to be sure

when nothing is ever for sure.

Which indeed is why

you mustn't close your eye

mustn't give up on the day,

today is not every day.

~

Don't worry about pleasing others right away;

they aren't all going to stay.

Worry about your mind

and worry about your spirit,

because that is what you'll find

to be there through and through.

Don't let it get turned into a maze,

and hard to get back to.

Smile

They told you to smile;

they did not want to see the face that hid your teeth.

They wanted a happy girl who was glad to be there,

teeth ready on command.

Dimples trained to be happy,

no one wanted to see the tears fallen on cheeks,

the teeth that showed in desperation,

dimples set in sadness.

A smile made by muscles being pulled,

trying to hold in depression.

Smile because you're happy,

because the photographer wants you to lie

don't smile because you're sad,

because life is treating you wrong.

Even so,

it is making you stronger.

Do not show those teeth,

unless words or phrases

have touched your soul.

Only the worthy should make you spread those lips.

Look happy when you are happy

not pretending or satisfying,

when you're ready and you're in love with a moment.

That is when pure joy should be seen.

~

A streak of pure attention

brings young ones to their feet.

Chivalry and kindness are

soon to be forgot,

all for the answer that you received in naught.

Words For What Is

Hey, I know it's been a while,

I tried to write a letter, but I didn't have the words to tell

I closed my eyes,

you did this to yourself

Now there's distance.

You broke the pavement with your footsteps,

leaving a trail of betrayal.

Just like Conor said, they're always changing sides.

You've made a semi-permanent destination,

a love sent to a wasteland.

You're still loved, always will be.

You know, you were my mentor,

and I'd like you to know that

you are never alone.

Know that you deserve to be happy,

I hope that you are.

Street Love

All the love of the street

rain is hanging out to dry,

cars run over hearts,

left to be scraped off the cement and clipped to a clothesline.

Modern art they call it.

Desperate smiles in need of an embrace,

stand in doorways and stare at the skies.

searching for a sunset

to bring along some hope.

Used up ashtrays left on patios and in backyards,

soon to be pummeled with ego and pride.

Unnecessary outlaws for the potentially hanging hearts,

To go with the hanging rain.

Drivers on roads, swollen without pity,

looking past the peacefulness

that could be within grasp.

Wet worlds and unremarked faith

don't want to be driven by a radical crowd.

Still want to have the believing

just not all those believers.

Blasphemy in its wake

as they preach about open arms

then go hide in their expensive shoes.

Hear the scraping of the hearts

all along the road

as everyone fights on in their battle.

Stardust Afternoon

Typos and band names,

She said stardust afternoon.

Shining lights and sparkling eyes

arrays of dazzling outcomes,

Action for action,

future consultations

party members at the bar

forgetting about their dreams.

Small talk turned into favors

pages drawn on while intact

A slip of the hand as she swipes on her eyeliner,

Try again

the future may hold a promise.

Earth Child

Out with nature

up amongst the trees,

mushrooms growing at my feet.

Searching for some fairy dust,

stubborn and stumbling

come now and take a rest.

The woods will carry you

the earth will guide you,

so long as your loyalty stays home.

Green is your home

oxygen is your medicine.

Do not give it up.

Ego and Criticizing

Judgement and drought,

Leave The Dreaming To The Flowers - Tiffiny Rose Allen

Silence is sometimes what will hear you

When it gets too loud.

Bury your hands into the dirt

find the answer in the stars.

Roll onto darkened grass

when the sun leaves for the day.

Take your crystals and wear them as a badge,

A duty to be kept.

Charge their energy by the moon

or charge them by the sea.

Then go and pray to your God

and seek more goodness.

Part VII

~Author's Note~

Love comes in many forms; it should be celebrated on any and every occasion. Love can be portrayed in over a million ways, and it deserves to be seen, whether that is in the forgiveness we provide, the rage when we face disappointment for loving so hard and so deeply, or simply in the purity and joy of it. Our ego, our beliefs, our way of living, our everything, all comes down to love, and the mystery of life.

Containing

Hope Of A Letter **237**

Influences **240**

Two Girls **242**

Lullaby **244**

Propaganda **246**

Your Awareness **250**

The Love Conversation **252**

I Promise You **254**

Open Heart **257**

Meadows **259**

Life Is A Short Ballad **261**

Sermon **263**

Future Textbooks **265**

Leave The Dreaming To The Flowers **267**

Love, Hold Dear **270**

Raise Your Head **272**

My Heart For You **274**

Positive Reinforcement **275**

Full Moon **277**

Sunflowers **280**

Temptation's Dread **283**

Word From The Ancient **284**

Love Advice **286**

Paint **288**

Don't Forget The Good **291**

Morose **294**

Beliefs **297**

Sitting By The Window **299**

Love's Artform **301**

Raindrop **303**

Sky **304**

Drive Safe **305**

For You **306**

~

I really love you, you know?

"I love you too."

~

Hope Of A Letter

Pass a letter to a son

he takes it, then moves on.

Onward to his partner

who sends it to her friend

passes it on to a cousin

who gives it to his sister,

takes it and hands it to a mister

Who hands it to them.

Onward and onward,

trailing through hands and reaching eyes,

pulling tears and tugging smiles.

Gets caught in a storm but finds a harbor,

Rainfall won't stop the light.

Leave The Dreaming To The Flowers - Tiffany Rose Allen

A small child picks it up from behind the shelter it had found,

opens the folds and looks at the words and smiles.

The hope of a letter lies in the child's hands,

and the child knows not how to read.

Giggling at the scribbled word they do not comprehend

folds it and molds it,

makes it anew

until they grow tired of the fragile paper

and drop it on the ground.

In mud and earth, it lays,

Days uncurling the shapes it was molded to.

Revealing ever so faintly the letters now,

"Darling dear, do not be afraid. I forgive you."

Perhaps those were the words.

Influences

The world says be an unbeliever,

but then they catch the holy fever

the fever of believers

who are actually deceivers

with a bunch of spoken seers

ready to throw in some coals.

They think they're right to throw you in a hole.

Medicine of a forecast,

time to gather all the outcasts

time to play the martyrdom of freedom

but there won't be any progress

if we keep dying where we lead them.

Maybe we can see them

The mediums of metaphysical premiums,

pay top dollar to tell you where you're going to go.

Your feet can answer that,

just remember to travel slow.

Shy intermediates,

want to let you know that they're leaving it,

out to find another reason

explore another season,

don't worry if they call you a heathen.

Search for your truth,

the path will be found behind your tooth,

remember to use an ice pack to soothe.

Leave The Dreaming To The Flowers - Tiffiny Rose Allen

Two Girls

Chasing shadows and the moon

two girls shaking what they got,

times won't be like this forever.

Aging out and letting in

the perils of the world.

Taking pictures, photographs

wonder how the time could stop.

Locked in memory, forever

Good times full of dancing

full of striking posing,

ranting and bitching

and all the in between.

Leave The Dreaming To The Flowers - Tiffiny Rose Allen

More good times to come,

for a good friendship pulls through,

two girls and the world,

You and me.

Leave The Dreaming To The Flowers - Tiffiny Rose Allen

Lullaby

Sacred days and broken plains,

feel that blood flow through those veins.

Finding nowhere in a dream

forget everything, from what we seem.

Girl said "Hey, I love you,"

don't go now

stay a few.

Sit down here right by my side,

forget about all those who lied.

It's okay to sit and cry

don't worry baby

I won't sigh.

To grow tired of you

is something I could never do.

If I find you in a nightmare

I'll take some of my paradise

and place it in your palms.

I hope the light will shine through

So I can see that smile again.

Selfish of me to demand your time,

But so much of my happiness resides with you,

it is with you.

Close those eyes and let me profess

How much you have lifted my loneliness.

If you go, I'll surely cry

I'll miss that sweet lullaby.

Propaganda

Eyes behold the ocean

Water so blue and waves so deep.

Yet you do not see the company it keeps.

Internet, media, newsstands, and stations.

Talk like they are preaching

believing and receiving

eyes feasting on the meals

of legends and false conceptions.

You can't believe science

you can't believe God,

you hide from it all

don't choose a side.

All the information is picked from a strawberry field

and fed to you in a shortcake

Leave The Dreaming To The Flowers - Tiffiny Rose Allen

rid of the green stem and the earth it was grown from.

Processed and overanalyzed

no purity left in it.

What could we believe

with all of this deceit?

Gullible and vulnerable,

wrapped up in brown paper bags.

Leaders laughing at the masses,

not sure of themselves

cause propaganda changed their thoughts

and images of themselves

the television got rid of core values.

Such is life for the common.

They say it is not noble

if you are without fare,

you don't work as hard

you don't try

you just sit back and waste.

For some of them, they work the hardest,

busting their asses and staying up late,

if only to put a meal on their child's plate.

World gone under

hasn't it always been?

Seek your own truths.

It is said again

and again it'll be said.

Seek. Your. Own. Truths.

'Cause in the end when it is

just you and your thoughts and yours and alone,

your individuality is what will see you through.

What's in that heart of yours is your salvation.

~

Crucifying criminals

and burying the edens.

Unwillingly cutting off their hair

then stealing from the poor.

Ethics, morals, kindness, strength.

What will it take to stand for what's right?

You can listen to the propaganda

and hope for the best,

but you might remain empty if you don't get up

and help out the rest.

The truth is not two solid colors,

it is one solid mind.

Your Awareness

Go on and fade away, why don't you?

Forget your past lives

until you need them again.

Take a journey and find a path

opening those eyes to what wasn't seen before.

Take a deep breath and let the words

flow through you.

The world is the same, the world is different.

Everyone remains in the same place except for you.

Forward, progress

words put on a page.

Loose leaf sentences

awaken the senses

don't heighten the noise.

Leave The Dreaming To The Flowers - Tiffiny Rose Allen

Things will make sense

things will reappear

all in good time.

Manifest the mystery

deep breath

the world is the same

the world is different.

The Love Conversation

One cannot choose whom they love.

It may seem a simple task

a path that should be etched into stone

but it is a tough road

a hard pact

not approved by all.

Love is an interesting entity

a wonder all its own

no words

no actions

can speak for it.

It is made to be interpreted

by the lovers who walk by it

only they can unlock

Leave The Dreaming To The Flowers - Tiffiny Rose Allen

what is meant to be

roaming through the sea of Galilee.

Predictions at its mark

days and ages caught between the two

A beautiful contradiction

bringing loveliness to its door.

I Promise You

I'm searching for a sign

I'm looking for an answer

but there aren't any answers

cause I'm a lost dimwit soul

who doesn't have any idea where to go.

One foot after the next,

That's what they'll tell you

Step after step you'll find your purpose,

I promise you.

That's what they'll tell you,

that's what they'll tell you.

Different states and frosting filled faces

Love's tenderness, boat in the storm.

Ask me my name, and I'll send back to you

Leave The Dreaming To The Flowers - Tiffiny Rose Allen

A telegram full of charms

To use for the moon.

Step after step

creation's afterlife,

all leading down the same road.

what is the quality of hate?

Sassafras makes root beer

in a landslide

shooting down the carbonated bubbles of entropy;

do the math

no one else will solve those problems.

Problems of the decade,

don't use too many numbers

solving a horizon

look for the sunset

there she goes

catch her before she falls

the moon is going to take over.

Gather all those crystals

charge them by the sea,

take hold of all and who you love

and do good by this world.

No one can save your soul but you.

Open Heart

Snowy days and spiritual dreams,

my heart is hanging off its seams.

Threadbare and open chest

Blood pumping,

you know the rest.

Open that heart up bare,

take it, it's all yours

gaze at all the secrets,

open the hidden doors.

Heart beating in your hand

yours to hold and understand.

Don't wander too far with it,

don't want the strings to snap.

Meadows

Do not hold yourself so low to the ground

unless you plan to take in

the fragrance of the wildflowers.

You are stardust in the air

you are lovely in the night.

When the sun shines on you,

you will close those eyes and fly.

No troubles present

you're alright,

take in the sweet perfume

of all that's not quite lost.

You've farther to go

and you will travel far,

Life will have its rewards

take them in as many as can be

and lift your eyelids for the dawn.

The grass is ever sweet and

no shadow can ensnare your beauty for long.

Life Is A Short Ballad

So much to focus on in this world,

there's love, hatred, war, peace,

and on and on the list can go.

Which is the one you choose to pour your energy into?

Which is the one to help you reach your fate and persevere?

Life is just a short ballad

play it so, and sweet

It will try to take the good out of us,

and maybe it will, for some

but we can try to not make it that way.

You can say I missed out,

a fine's feather for a pound.

You can say those nights dancing

Leave The Dreaming To The Flowers - Tiffiny Rose Allen

in front of the moon were meaningless,

that gowns and booze

make a time worth having.

My time has always been worth having,

so long as it's with you.

Sermon

Go to church, pray to God

come back home and walk in nature

then pray to the earth and see it through.

Let's sit down and meditate

brush the world's influence away

and go astray

Let's be witches after church

Not heeding to the words of the holy leaders

that preacher ain't my teacher

He's not accustomed or higher to me.

In my moment, I will show it

and my powers will be free,

soft and subtle

I'll be gentle

say your verses,

I still believe.

I still believe.

You were just the one who thought

I would revoke the sun

when instead you let the devil in yourself.

Future Textbooks

Take a seat and listen dear

may we annihilate this fear.

Let subjective criticism lie away

all the elements shall provide.

She laid in grass and laughed all day

she touched the delicate ground

her necklaces held crystals

for healing, for help.

Maybe the people laughed,

maybe they mocked

perhaps the opinions were uncalled for

invalid in her state of mind,

no concern given

Leave The Dreaming To The Flowers - Tiffiny Rose Allen

for she knew her place.

She knew her way,

walked by it in the soundest mind.

Not everyone can collide,

not all who see hold accuracy,

Let's pave the way in stone.

The moon shines down, blessing the world

Night being seen as the darkest of paths

sun is innocent with its rays

No one questions the authority

Sleep comes at the crack of sunset

and history is prolonged.

cause day by day we get closer

to ending up in a textbook,

even if it is just an appearance.

Leave The Dreaming To The Flowers

The world is out to get you,

it's going to show you joy, and it is going to rip you apart.

Don't let it rip you apart.

Just leave the dreaming to the flowers, love.

Don't waste your time in worry and ambition, love.

The world is going to show you happiness

it is going to cause you to worry

don't let it cause you to worry.

Go out with the flowers, love.

Don't wrench them of their youth,

Sit and pet the petals gently, love.

Look at that perfection, look at that beauty.

Leave The Dreaming To The Flowers - Tiffiny Rose Allen

Leave the dreaming to the flowers,

They'll be alright with them.

Don't let your mind be scolded,

cruel words told by you for you

aren't going to help you out.

Take your thoughts and leave them in the fields,

let the fragrances and the wind carry it all away.

You go ahead,

walk back to the civilized and the professional.

Knotted hair and dirty feet

aren't permitted in the towns

they're told to wash themselves or stay outside.

Let me tell you,

stay outside because that is where your peace will grow.

Leave The Dreaming To The Flowers - Tiffiny Rose Allen

Leave the dreaming to the flowers,

Just go and fly in the breeze.

You'll get sad looks as they think they're feeling bad for you,

But you need not pay them any mind.

Hanging on to the burden of past memories and ambitions

They held too tightly,

didn't provide enough leverage,

now they're stuck with some carpeted rooms

invading their minds and becoming dark.

No fresh air or flowers scent.

Leave the dreaming to the flowers,

They'll make due with your wandering.

Love, Hold Dear

Sweet sincere,

love, hold dear.

Time will try to hurry

minutes will flash by

unscathed and cordially,

clock's hand counting down

fierce coincide with mortal wishes,

won't let them get ahead.

Trouble's mayhem may ensue,

opinions and tricks thrown out

may the curses of the world

cease and let joy be.

Forgiveness is a premise for construct

criticism left at the door,

Leave The Dreaming To The Flowers - Tiffiny Rose Allen

go inside and sit gladly

all shall be made well,

For a dreamer's heart is overflown

and someday is not set in stone.

Raise Your Head

Raise your head tonight,

take in the clouds

look at those stars.

You're beautiful like them, you know

a beautiful star flake,

hanging around the sky

talking to the clouds

sticking it out even when the sun outshines you.

Glistening star dandruff

shooting across the atmosphere,

sun and moon claim to be the main attractions

but who would they be without

that sparkle behind their eyes?

Sugar coated gases,

dipped in a bowl of glitter,

you rise so far beyond

those thoughts that rise in you.

Raise your head tonight,

look at those stars.

You're beautiful like them, you know.

My Heart For You

Looking at you now

so distantly,

I have no more anger

in my heart for you.

For the anger was only within me,

and now I must let you go.

Positive Reinforcement

Our goals come in fractions

they begin a little at a time.

Our aspirations, our to-do lists, our goals,

carved and conceived,

worked on like intricate fishing poles,

want to manifest and make beliefs come true,

no wonder valid unless you can prove it.

What is the purpose of a dream unless you can achieve it?

No prediction is going to cause a reaction;

no energy source is going to help out the process,

just rigorous challenging work and the atheistic knowledge of magic.

The world won't help you unless you let it.

If dreams don't live, then it wasn't meant to be,

or it's just not time yet.

Leave The Dreaming To The Flowers - Tiffany Rose Allen

Don't blame it on the world,

don't blame it on the sound,

keep the enchanting in your heart.

Your apostrophes are just placing pauses in your soul,

your matter is divulging,

don't break it down.

If your plans don't work out,

a path will open for you,

no life is insufficient.

Perhaps they're right when they say it will work out,

it will work out

if you're open to the outcome.

Full Moon

Full moon tonight,

Isn't it pretty?

All orange in hue and adorned in the sky,

hung like an ornament,

just for your eyes.

Crossing the star of

purpose and change,

time for a beginning, time for an ending.

I am like a crushed soufflé

I was sad yesterday,

now it makes sense

full moons always bring out these emotions.

Prepared now

I can walk through,

Leave The Dreaming To The Flowers - Tiffiny Rose Allen

take what comes this way

and walk on,

until the next moon comes,

until the next change rises.

For change is a path

and yet ever flowing,

can make all look and remain the same,

through exact times showing nothing is as it was.

~

I wish to find you where no one can,

but where all can see.

I wish to find you for every truth,

I wish to find you so that I can understand

so that others can take this journey.

So, I can join them and they can join me,

in a lesson of life and all.

Sunflowers

Potassium records,

banana mashed up,

walks with the sunflowers

unveiled before they wither

petal by petal

show a sunflower's blood.

Miniature garden

'til it grows up

shooting skyward until it's cut down

words cut like a blade

cut it all down 'til your ego turns high.

Sapphire sweethearts

not all are blue

turn them to red, some yellow, some purple,

Leave The Dreaming To The Flowers - Tiffiny Rose Allen

like the flower you tread.

Bright and sunny until you say those words.

You say whore love, whore love,

You say superficial breast implants

stitched together for a pretty penny then fucked until I have to go back,

Whore love.

Maybe you're grand under your tomb

placed like a mannequin

set for your purpose...

Maybe you weren't there to decide for yourself

Maybe that's why your words fall and demean

Blood falls from petals as flowers fall to the ground

Sun lowers and nutrients goes,

moonlight may be getting through

by the time dawn insists on showing

new seeds will have been sown.

Temptation's Dread

Hell's going to ring and the devil

wants to sing you a tempted lullaby

to silence your painful cry,

from the night you threw it all away

and didn't want to stay,

Now damning your eternal worth

left alone back in the dirt.

Redemption was a key,

Now, your philosophy is surely worn out.

Word From The Ancient

Cleopatra was an artist,

her beauty was a view,

people came to see her

and she smiled with grandeur.

Ancient icons and their beginnings

get objectified by a war

of mass completion and rumor markets

standing outside of doors.

Trying to sell newspapers,

talking about analytical past tenses,

pterodactyls flew to somewhere

and rexes grew too old.

Dinosaurs need painkillers

and advanced survival skills.

Throw away your ghosts and look at what is here.

Spirits will collide and drop hints,

take them as you need them.

Love Advice

It's not how you love, it's how you fly.

How you soar, how you learn

how you push on through the rain.

Love is not a word made up of simple letters.

It is an everlasting feeling

that can rip you to pieces

as soon as you've felt it.

It is good and evil and everything that makes the two.

Without the accompaniment of trust,

love cannot have two hearts, only one,

Single columned and double-jointed.

Rejoice,

for love has found you in many ways.

~

I'm glad to be on your side,

I'm glad to have eyes that see you.

With your aura made of blue,

with everything that I consist of,

I love you.

Paint

The liquid's thick,

It lies in circular walls,

A brush dips in, then paints away

it's rhythmic tune, covering all our sins.

We live in it, we breathe in it, we are smothered in it.

It rains, it pours, it consumes.

This thickness we cannot swallow,

we try to move but it only coats us,

we are lathered by this paint.

The rhythmic brush as it covers our sins

That rhythmic tune as it shapes our lives

Painting our portraits,

choosing the melody.

Leave The Dreaming To The Flowers - Tiffiny Rose Allen

Mixing and creating shades of light and dark,

Is there any way to step out of this canvas?

I am drowning in this fault

my hands they cannot reach the air.

Trying to swim through this vile color,

Changing the shades as I go.

All I desire is to create my own;

my sins do not need hiding,

I know just what I do.

Remove your brush

for my paint is my own choice.

My canvas will be how I desire,

to be tossed in the rain

hoping to be cleansed of your coats.

~

Fretful days go unnoticed,

ugly meets ugly as pain shatters art.

Creating beauty from irony.

Don't Forget The Good

I know things are fucked up,

I know things might not be

how we want them to be.

I know I've stood tall all on my own,

I was betrayed by ones I've loved,

I was left when I was confident in a friend.

Who could be a friend if you left me on the steps?

They told me not to choose sides

we can live with one another,

but I know that's just not right

it's now how we are going to love each other.

Why can't everyone I love, love each other?

You're stuck in the past

you're trying to move forward

but holding onto hatred for the ones who love you

isn't how you're going to heal.

I used to wonder why we always hurt the ones we love,

why do we push them away and hate ourselves?

I think it is a grand mixture

between not feeling deserving

and not wanting to do any hurting,

but in trying to avoid conflict,

you're just going to cause more bruises.

My experience, at least.

I'll love you until you can love yourself.

I'll love you even if you can't,

but I'm not sure I'm even capable

of having enough love for myself.

Everyone is stuck in a rift

everyone hates the same person.

Ourselves.

Leave The Dreaming To The Flowers - Tiffiny Rose Allen

We're not rooting for ourselves

we're stuck in the in between

the good and the bad,

and I guess that's okay,

as long as we don't forget the good.

Morose

Sugared caramel daydreams,

added to the list of beauty queens

all obsessed with their things

hair primped up to fit the theme,

I wonder why nothing seems,

to be full reality.

Though it's touched,

my mind searches for an answer

but subconscious is so stubborn,

I can't find the maniacal payroll

that injures my process of thinking.

Why was I so busy dreaming?

Everyone is getting tickets to the stage

while I'm stuck here

sitting on the edge

pondering my life

don't give in to strife,

rub the pain away,

just for an hour,

tired of this taste so sour.

Gorgeous anecdote,

I seize the remote,

but the batteries died out,

now I'm left with my shout

'cause we're left with evil seekers

caught in the pain of medieval,

throw away a key

everything he's said to him is gospel.

Leave The Dreaming To The Flowers - Tiffiny Rose Allen

Lock the door and go and prosper,

But what you don't figure

is that where we linger

sometimes allows being right in the end,

cause your prophecies are only

the nominees of a false organization,

cut and bleed from a clothespin.

don't accuse the ones who are abused,

seek redemption in your sleep.

Beliefs

She's seen the fire

darkened embers lit up like lightbulbs,

coal shining like an invitation

come closer 'til you're damned.

Angel's lights shine a different light,

not mysterious, not suspicious,

walk in that holy line

yet they don't seem so holy.

Pray to a higher power,

put all energy towards that illumination.

Nothing wrong with that,

pray to your holy spirit

don't criticize the ones who don't.

Everyone flees until they must fight

Leave The Dreaming To The Flowers - Tiffiny Rose Allen

Face your worries and let go,

you're better off that way,

and it's okay to pray about it.

Sitting By The Window

The

Room is dull,

the only light is

the sun rays from the blinds.

Tea in hand

have a seat

the shadows start to play

revealing so much disarray

but eyes only look on

ignoring the shapes and figures through the glass.

The window pane,

unique clusters of cutlery

make themselves known,

but eyes only look on

Leave The Dreaming To The Flowers - Tiffiny Rose Allen

not looking up to see the chaos.

A smile is shed as someone cries out,

yet no one looks up,

instead, they refill their cup

taking in the company of all the aristocrats.

No mind for the lowly,

Someday it will be known

That those cups are overflowing

and gluttony is a sin.

Love's Artform

Love may well be the greatest artform in all of humanity.

God is the greatest artist,

to make and design such complex pieces,

to fit together in a form, purest

hope that such feeling never ceases.

No one is a blank canvas,

alone you are your own picture,

together you create a landmass.

Who could've discovered such a mixture

Found those colors so bold, so great?

Such a view is not for taking

but seeing

side by side.

The grandest art piece known to us

For such a love to abide

and stick around awhile

for the greatest art these eyes have seen

must've been that smile.

~

Art is the gateway to every dream and thought we've had.

Love may be the best form of art we have with us.

Raindrop

You look like something worth looking at for a while.

Plain and simple,

yet so clear,

like a raindrop

resting on a petal

so sweet

and so sincere.

All this rain and all this beauty

I wonder if the clouds know

what they've made.

Sky

When the sky turns into a painting

that's when we realize our place.

Abstract figures in an art piece,

hoping to be known

to make some kind of statement

loudly or quietly

more or less the same.

Drive Safe

I say, 'Drive safe' because if I don't

I feel like something bad could happen.

I say, 'Drive safe' because that reminder could save your life.

I say, 'Drive safe' because I don't want any harm to come you.

I say it because it shows how much I care for you.

'Drive safe' isn't just those two words,

it is an eternity.

Because if I can't be there to tell you myself,

at least this message could pull through.

Drive safe, not only because your life could depend on it,

but because if I don't say it, my life could surely cease.

So, drive safe, for me, and for you.

For You

I hope that you learn to love yourself,

someday.

I hope that you learn that you are beyond your flaws.

You are more than you think and you deserve to be

liked, to be loved.

You deserve to let go of your past,

even when it haunts you

especially when it haunts you.

I hope you learn to move on from your mistakes,

to not mind some of the words you say.

I hope you learn that it is okay to let the tears fall

to not repress, it is okay to not repress

it is a hard habit to be broken.

Try not to overthink

Leave The Dreaming To The Flowers - Tiffiny Rose Allen

don't focus on the dark side.

Try not to care what those people think of you

what all of those people think of you.

Just another face in the crowd,

that person who is there with no particular opinion.

Don't care what they think.

They are not up to you to like you

you are up to you to like you.

I hope you learn that some things can't change

and some of the things that can are going to be

the hardest, and they're going to try to

take everything out of you.

I hope that you try to accept this

and not let it beat you

because no matter what,

no matter what they say

it is not up to them

you are never up to them.

You don't have to be.

Toxic is not family, it is not friendship, and it is not community

It is poison.

Do not let the venom consume the marrow of your bones.

I hope you learn that it is okay to live.

It is okay to be you.

~

You are not up to them,

You are up to you.

~

AFTERWORD

Thank you for sharing space with my words, I hope you have enjoyed them. I do not expect the pages that you have read to be of total perfection, I believe that there is a beauty in flaws that perfection could never understand, and the absence of flaws would surely mean I have no place among humankind. The multitude of poems contained within these pages vary and portray so many different emotions and themes, and at their center they represent what growing into a woman has been like for me.

To kind of wrap everything within these pages together, I felt called to create a song for this collection, something that embodies every word and every feeling. It is titled the same as this book, and if you feel so called, I would be honored if you listened to it.

I wanted to write a lullaby, a slightly haunting ordeal, but one that was full of hope at the same time. If you listen closely, there are lots of nature themes thrown in, crickets, crows, birdsong, ocean waves, and waterfalls. I wanted this piece to delicately and vibrantly connect with nature, I wanted the sounds of the earth to be wrapped up and strewn throughout it, providing a sense of connection to all that there is.

I think that every aspect of life contains poetry, the simplest things can turn into our muses, a beautiful sunset can say more than any line or phrase of the human word, and I can only hope that I have done the earth some justice in my expression of it all.

To conclude, I just want to say how grateful I am to have shared all of the things that have moved me, and provoked a written line, for it allows me to remember that beauty is contained within everything.

Leave The Dreaming To The Flowers - Tiffiny Rose Allen

Leave the Dreaming to the Flowers

Lyrics

My flower garden was being trampled
I stumbled and I fell as I tried
to collect the weeds
and place them elsewhere.

I offered up my heart but it got uprooted,
the strings becoming tangled and misshapen as they
bruised.

My little melancholy muse,
allowing no longer the darkness and deceit,
So often placing the blame on me

I will not be unhappy, I refuse, I refuse, I refuse

They said leave the dreaming to the flowers
they'll be alright with them

Leave your dreams at the flowerbeds
so you can go and live them
The flowers will dream for you

as you live the life you wished for

Leave the dreaming to the flowers
Leave the dreaming to the flowers

they'll be alright with them

they'll be alright with them.

Leave The Dreaming To The Flowers - Tiffiny Rose Allen

ABOUT THE AUTHOR

Tiffiny Rose Allen is a writer and poet. Originally from the state of Florida, she started writing at an early age and self-published her first collection of poetry *Leave The Dreaming To The Flowers* at the age of 18. Her poetry is eclectic in portraying her views of the different aspects of life. When she is not somewhere writing, she is either creating something with her hands or working on anything and everything that excites her. Her work has been featured in numerous magazine and anthology publications, including *The Elpis Pages, Harness Magazine,* and *Dreamer by Night Magazine*. Her poetry and short story collections can be found on Amazon.

You can find more of her work on Instagram @dreamsinhiding.writing or on her website at https://dreamsinhiding.wixsite.com/mysite.

Leave The Dreaming To The Flowers - Tiffiny Rose Allen

Also By Tiffiny Rose Allen

Leave The Dreaming To The Flowers (2017)

Tell The Monster Who You Are (2018)

A Rainbow Against A Darkened Sky (2019)

Canorous: Words Written In The Age Of Social Distancing (2020)

The Parables Of A Hopeful Life Seeker: Or Just Another Collection Of Shadow Work (2020)

We Are Based Off Our Dreamscapes (2021)

Leave The Dreaming To The Flowers - Tiffiny Rose Allen